KIDS
making
QUILTS
for
KIDS

◆◆◆

BY ABC QUILTS

◆

A young person's guide for having fun while helping others

and learning about AIDS and substance abuse

THE QUILT DIGEST PRESS

Published in the United States of America by The Quilt Digest Press.

Editorial and production direction by Bill Folk.
Cover copy by Sharon Gilbert.
Editing by Jan Johnson.
Book and cover design by Kajun Graphics, San Francisco.
Cover photography by Sharon Beals, San Francisco.
Quilt photography by Sharon Risedorph, San Francisco.
All other photographs courtesy of ABC Quilts or as credited.
Diagrams and illustrations by Kandy Petersen.
Typographical composition by DC Typography, San Francisco.
Printing by Nissha Printing Company Ltd., Kyoto, Japan.
Color separations by the printer.

Special thanks to Kandy Petersen and Holly Smith for the time and talent they donated to this project.
Our gratitude to ABC Quilts for trusting us with this special project and for the opportunity to contribute to the wonderful work they do.

First Printing

ISBN 0-913327-36-0

Library of Congress Cataloging-in-Publication Data

Kids making quilts for kids: a young person's guide for having fun while helping others and learning about AIDS and substance abuse / by ABC Quilts.
    p.   cm.
  Summary: Contains instructions for making quilts to be given to children suffering from AIDS or problems related to substance abuse. Also includes a section of facts and myths about these conditions.
  ISBN 0-913327-36-0 : $9.95
  1. Quilting — Patterns — Juvenile literature.   2. AIDS (Disease) in children — Juvenile literature.   3. Infants — Effect of drugs on — Juvenile literature.   (1. Quilting.   2. AIDS (Disease)   3. Drug abuse.   4. Handicraft.)   I. ABC Quilts (Organization)
TT835.K488   1992   91-48338
746.9'7 — dc20   CIP
                                                         AC

The Quilt Digest Press
P.O. Box 1331
Gualala, California 95445

TABLE OF CONTENTS

ACKNOWLEDGMENTS

ABC Quilts would like to thank all the hundreds of contributors to this book project. In particular, we'd like to thank Janet Ahlgren for working with Ellen in writing and developing this book; Helen Kushnick, whose support provided the fuel for the organization and basic equipment like the computers and copiers we used while writing the manuscript; Geneva Woodruff for being the enthusiastic visionary that she is; Joann Bailey for her special insights into quilting; Jacquie McDonald and Karen Reist for providing invaluable support and advice; Newman's Own for sponsoring the development effort; Fred Rockefeller of Cranston Printworks for encouragement and support from the beginning; Sue Robertson and her 4-H Club boys; Laura Guinan for her behind the scenes contributions; Ruby Transue for continuing to help in more and more ways; all the makers of the quilts pictured in this book; Ann White for all the tangible and intangible ways she helps on a daily basis; Clarence Ahlgren and our families for taking up the slack; Helen Weiman and Jane Smith for ongoing support; and all the quilters and other volunteers who carry out the mission of ABC Quilts every day in every state.

We'd also like to thank the many educators and health professionals who have talked with us extensively about the factual information in the "Discussion Starters" section, especially the National Council on Alcoholism and Drug Dependence, Inc. (NCADD); the Prevention and Training Center of the Mt. Auburn Hospital; the National Institute on Drug Abuse (NIDA); and the Departments of Public Health in Massachusetts, New York, and California.

And last, but certainly not least, we are most grateful to Bill Folk and the entire Quilt Digest Press production team for their commitment to this project and for their assistance in making our first publishing attempt turn into a beautiful book!

Introduction
WELCOME TO THE ABC QUILT PROJECT

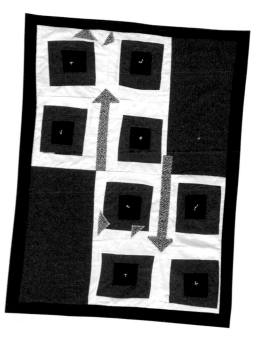

Riverside Junior High School
Springfield, Vermont

We at ABC Quilts want to tell you the story about how the idea of making baby quilts to comfort sick children has mushroomed into a huge nationwide project. And we want to invite you to become part of this project. It's easy, and it's fun. And you'll have the satisfaction of knowing that you've done something for someone else.

This book is designed to help you join our effort to make a quilt for every child born infected with the HIV/AIDS virus or born with birth defects caused by alcohol, cocaine, or other harmful drugs. Many of these children are "boarders" who live in hospitals or other institutions because their families can't care for them or they are homeless. In fact, we find the children to give the quilts to through these institutions. As of this printing, there are more than 100,000 of these children in this country alone. And more around the world.

Because so many people want to get involved and have asked for easy-to-follow directions for making a quilt, we've created this book. We hope you have fun using it!

Back in 1988, in the small town of Northwood, New Hampshire, a retired school teacher and counselor, named Ellen Ahlgren, read an article in a newsletter written by a doctor, Elisabeth Kübler-Ross. Dr. Kübler-Ross told about the thousands of babies who were living out their short lives within the walls of hospitals because they had been born infected with the HIV/AIDS virus and their families couldn't care for them. (By reading this book, you can find out how babies can be born addicted to drugs or HIV-infected.)

Mrs. Ahlgren's heart went out to these little ones. She decided to do something special for them. She wanted to give them something of their very own. She remembered how much fun her own grandchildren had with the quilts she'd made for them. Quilts are snuggly and comforting. And they're fun to drag around and play with.

An idea was born! What if all the quilters in this country made a quilt and sent it to these little kids? Wouldn't that be a great way to send them some love and comfort? To show them that someone cared about them?

Mrs. Ahlgren talked to her family and friends about her idea. They all said, "Let's go for it!" They asked people at hospitals what size the quilts should be and what fabrics would work well. (Since hospitals use industrial laundries, the fabric must be sturdy.) Then they made up some flyers and printed hundreds of them to get the word out. Everyone took a few to fabric and quilting stores, to schools, groups, and churches. Soon people all over the Northeast started making baby quilts.

Newspapers and television stations heard about this story, and they spread the word across the country and around the world—like wildfire. Boys and girls like you—as well as teachers, group leaders, parents, grandparents, and other adults—have made thousands of quilts. Some get involved through their schools, Scout troops, Sunday school classes, 4-H clubs, and other youth organizations. Some just work alone or with a few of their friends.

From July 1988 through July 1989, the ABC Quilt Project delivered 500 quilts to kids. In the next year, they made and gave away 2,200 quilts. And in the next year people made 22,000—ten times as many! Every year we need more and more quilts.

The numbers of children born HIV-positive or affected by alcohol or drugs are increasing every day. At first, we thought we had more quilts than places to send them. Now we know we don't have enough baby quilts to meet the needs of hospitals, day care centers, and foster care homes caring for these sick kids. Unfortunately, we'll always need more quilts.

We need everyone's help to make sure that all of these children receive their own cozy, comfy little ABC quilt. If you decide to join our effort, be sure to ask for help from your teacher, your parents, your group leader, or an experienced quilter. They'll probably be happy to help you and might even make a quilt too. (Teens, we know you can do it by yourself. And, if you have some experience sewing, you might consider helping some younger kids make a quilt too.)

Many letters come to us every week from hospitals telling stories of how much the kids love their quilts. One four-year-old boy, who has to travel a long way on the train every week to receive his treatment, always carries his quilt with him. Many children go to their "needle-stick" treatment at the hospital hugging their quilts tight to their chests. They feel the love and comfort that's sewn into each one.

You can make a difference by making a special quilt for one of these kids. In the following pages are the directions for making the quilts and getting them to ABC Quilts who will distribute your quilt to children who need them.

Good luck!
Love to all of you,
The ABC Quilts Staff

Chapter 1
GETTING STARTED

A quilt is a bedcovering that has three layers:

1. The *face*, also called the top or front, is usually decorated in some way.
2. The *filling*, or batting, is the fluffy layer in between the face and the back. The filling makes the quilt feel soft and cozy and keeps the children warm.
3. The *back* is made of a fabric that is similar to or coordinates with the face.

WHAT KIND OF FABRIC IS BEST?

Be sure the fabric you choose for the face and back layers of your ABC Quilt is mostly cotton for softness and tightly woven so it can withstand frequent, repeated washings in a hospital's heavy-duty laundry. Keep in mind that many sick babies are allergic to synthetic fabrics (like polyester or nylon). We recommend 100% cotton or a mostly cotton-polyester blend containing at least 50% cotton.

WHAT KIND OF FILLING IS BEST?

We recommend light or medium-weight bonded polyester batting for ABC Quilts. This will best withstand repeated washing. Pre-quilted fabric may also be used for the back, but it's more expensive. Some people like to use one layer of cotton flannel for the filling. This makes a nice lightweight quilt.

WHERE DO YOU BEGIN?

First you'll choose a design for your quilt. There are four different designs in this booklet—a block quilt, a traditional patchwork quilt, a block and lattice quilt, and a creative quilt. Read through the instructions and choose the one that appeals to you. If you've never made a quilt or done any sewing before, you'll want to

Sunday School
Asbury United Methodist Church
Chesterfield, New Hampshire

choose the printed panel quilt or the traditional patchwork quilt. They're simpler to start with. And, remember, you can always make more than one.

Choosing the size will depend somewhat on your design and somewhat on the age of the baby or child you wish to make a quilt for. A good size for newborns is approximately 36″ by 36″. For children two to six years old a good size is approximately 38″ by 44″ or so. We've recommended sizes with each of the quilt designs.

Planning your quilt is the most important step in quiltmaking. Good planning takes practice and time. Take the time to carefully plan your quilt colors and design. Work with graph paper for accuracy. You can even color in the parts so you have a better idea what your quilt will look like. You will often refer to your plan as you are making your quilt. We've included some templates (to-size patterns) for parts of some of the quilts for you.

Choosing your colors and fabrics can be lots of fun. Quilts are a lot like paintings. They combine many colors and shapes and figures, arranged in designs that result in harmony and balance. Bright colors are stimulating and attract attention. Pastels are soothing. Large prints and shapes contrast with small ones for balance. Be creative!

Before you begin working on a quilt, collect all your fabrics and materials. Remember to use 100% cotton (or a cotton-polyester blend) fabric. Be sure to wash, dry, and press all fabric before you cut it. This removes the fabric treatment called "sizing" and allows for possible shrinkage. Please don't use knit fabrics. They stretch and they don't stand up to repeated washing so they do not work well for ABC Quilts.

The amount of fabric you buy will depend on the size quilt you want to make. Remember you'll need extra fabric to allow for borders, seams, shrinkage, and quilt back. The filling, or batting, can be bought by the yard or in precut crib-sized packages. Refer to the specific design you choose for exact yardage information.

4H Club, "The Wise Owls"
Auburn, New Hampshire

ASSEMBLING YOUR EQUIPMENT
- ◆ sharp scissors (scissors for fabric need to be sharper than scissors for paper)
- ◆ sewing machine, bobbins, thread, and needles
- ◆ quilt pins (long ones with round glass heads, so they don't get lost in the quilt. Imagine snuggling up to a surprise pin!)

METRIC CONVERSION TABLE

The amount of fabric needed for quilts and other measurements in this book are given in yards and inches. If you are accustomed to metric measurements, you can use this conversion chart to figure lengths. For instance, if the quilt calls for 2½ yards, you'll need just over 2¼ meters (2.275 to be precise).

1 meter	=	1 yard, 3.4 inches
1 yard	=	.91 meters
1 decimeter	=	3.94 inches
1 centimeter	=	.39 inches
1 inch	=	2.54 centimeters

- thread and needles for basting and hand sewing
- ruler and yardstick
- iron and ironing board
- embroidery cotton or crochet cotton to match fabric, for tying
- embroidery needles with long eyes, for embroidery or crochet thread
- thimble
- permanent fabric marking pen for your autograph on back corner of quilt (For the block and lattice and creative quilts, you'll need some other supplies. See pages 19 and 25.)

A LITTLE PRE-QUILT PRACTICE

Practice stitching ¼″ seams for accuracy. Use a piece of 8½″ by 11″ blue lined notebook paper and a sewing machine with a general purpose presser foot and *no thread.* (The presser foot is that metal piece that looks like a foot. That foot and your hands hold the fabric in place as you sew.) Lift the presser foot, and place one sheet of paper under the presser foot so that the needle will pierce the first blue line. Lower the presser foot. Hold the paper with both hands, one on each side and a little in front of the foot, to guide the blue line toward the needle.

Don't watch the needle. Use the edge on the right side of the presser foot as a guide. The right half of a presser foot is about ¼″ wide, and you'll be training your eye to sew a straight ¼″ seam allowance. Your quilt will look a whole lot better if you can sew a straight seam. Your aim is to fill the sheet with stitching holes (still no thread) exactly on each blue line.

Stitch slowly and carefully, staying right on the line. Be very careful to keep your fingers away from the needle. (It could easily go through your finger accidentally. If this happens, *do not* pull your finger away. Call for help.)

Practice controlling the speed of the sewing machine so you can stitch straight lines. Practice guiding the paper so your stitches fall precisely on the blue lines. This small amount of practice will help you when you're stitching with thread on fabric.

If you've never done any sewing by hand, practice hand stitching as well. Work with a scrap of cloth or an old sheet and thread of a contrasting color so you can see your stitches. There are three basic stitches you'll need for these quilts—basting, which is large (2″) temporary stitches; running stitches if you are going to hand-quilt (the same as basting only much smaller); and blind stitches, a hidden stitch to close your quilt up once the parts are attached to each other.

To baste you simply move the needle up and down in long running stitches, beginning on the bottom. To do the running stitch you take smaller even stitches. The stitches should be the same size on both sides of the fabric. To do the blind stitch you move the needle back and forth in small even stitches underneath a fold. See Diagram 1.

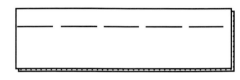

Basting stitch

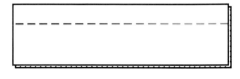

Running stitch

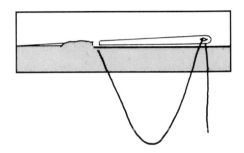

Blind stitch

Diagram 1

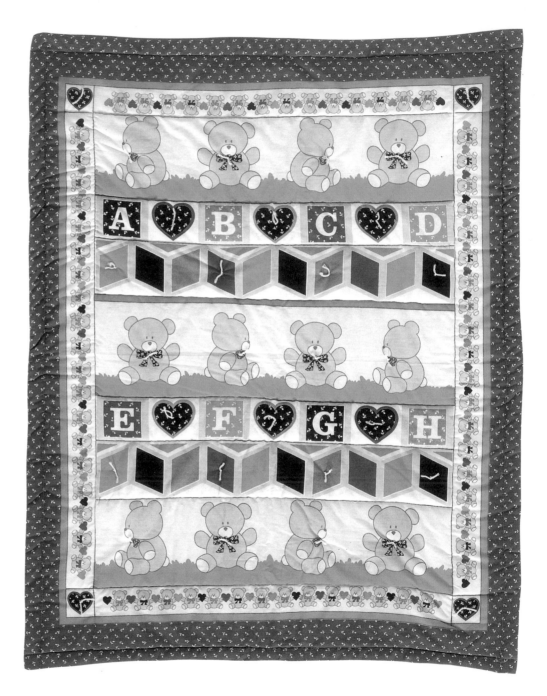

PRINTED PANEL QUILT

▲▲▲
12

Chapter 2
FOUR DIFFERENT QUILT FACES

This chapter is divided up into four sections, one for each of the quilt-top designs. Remember, the first two are simpler. You'll want to begin with one of them and then maybe try another more complicated one.

THE PRINTED PANEL QUILT

A panel with a pre-printed design can be the beginning of a lovely quilt that's easy to make. Making a quilt like this is a good way to get some practice quilting.

Often the panel is printed with all the borders printed on the sides. Cut these borders from the sides, and sew them onto the top and bottom edges to create a quilt with the correct proportions. Some designs have no extra borders.

The design should appear lengthwise, the top of the design near the baby's head and the bottom of the design near the baby's feet. The quilt should either be square or longer than it is wide.

MATERIALS
- One printed panel for the quilt face, or front, usually 45″ wide, 36″ long, if the fabric has a border. An all-over print can simply be cut to the size you choose. Choose a print you think would please a small child.
- One piece of fabric the same size as the front panel in a coordinating color for the quilt back.

- One piece of batting the same size as the face panel, for the inside layer. (Using pre-quilted material for the back eliminates the need for batting.)
- Thread to match the quilt face background color.

Note: Printed panel fabric is usually 45″ wide. Most panels run across the width and require about 1 yard or 1¼ yards for the complete design. On some fabrics the design runs lengthwise. Since printed fabric varies so much, get some expert advice at the fabric store on how much fabric to buy for the design you choose.

Refer to Steps 1 through 5 in The Eight Basic Steps of Making an ABC Quilt on page 33. First, you sew the facing and backing together. Then you add the filling.

By sewing ¼″ seams all around to attach the quilt face, filling and back, the finished quilt will be approximately 35″ by 44″, a good size for a quilt for an older child.

Consult the section on Adding Borders for more complete instructions on how to handle borders, if you choose to add some to your quilt.

When your quilt is assembled, refer to Steps 6 through 8 on how to finish your quilt. The easiest way to quilt is to tie the quilt. If you have a simple print, quilting around flowers or dinosaurs (or whatever is in the print) either by hand or machine can make the quilt extra fancy.

THE TRADITIONAL PATCHWORK QUILT

Traditional patchwork designs can be simple or very complicated. We'll show you a design that's fun for beginners. Many other types of traditional designs are more appropriate for students with advanced sewing experience. First master basic quilting skills, and later as you become more experienced at quilting, you won't feel frustrated when you move to these more complicated designs.

This patchwork quilt of 6″ blocks is arranged in a pattern of six across by six down, a total of thirty-six blocks. These can be assembled from a wide variety of colors and patterns of fabrics. (Remember to use a blend that is at least half cotton or use 100% cotton.) Or you can purchase fabric in just a few complementary colors and designs. Blocks can be made from any size, of course, depending on the fabric you have available. (Some quilters make beautiful patchwork from squares

Cub Scouts Pack 129, Den 4
Perry, Maine

TRADITIONAL PATCHWORK QUILT

1	2	3	4	5	6	Row 1
7	8	9	10	11	12	Row 2
13	14	15	16	17	18	Row 3
19	20	21	22	23	24	Row 4
25	26	27	28	29	30	Row 5
31	32	33	34	35	36	Row 6

Diagram 2

To Make Your Patchwork Quilt

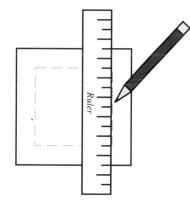

Diagram 3

as small as 1″, but this means a lot more cutting and sewing.) For your first quilt, use the template we've included in this book.

This quilt, made by Cub Scout Pack 129, Den 4 in Perry, Maine, is made with two main colors A and B, and uses the same color B for the borders and back. Whatever design you choose, and however many colors you decide on, be sure to plan your design with a pencil on graph paper before you start cutting. This is very important, because you'll refer to this plan many times as you put your quilt together. Draw the quilt to scale and color your design according to your fabric choices. This will allow you to estimate how much yardage of each fabric you'll need. Adjust colors and fabrics until your design pleases you. Number the blocks across each row, starting in the upper left corner, as shown in Diagram 2.

Count the number of blocks of each color in your design, to decide how much fabric to buy. Use another piece of graph paper to lay out a cutting chart for each color of fabric in your quilt. Plan to buy a little extra fabric to allow for shrinkage and those little mistakes we all make sometimes.

Be sure to wash, dry, and press all fabric before measuring and cutting, because some fabrics shrink and some are treated with fabric finishes called sizing, which must be removed by washing.

MATERIALS
For the quilt shown (approximately 40″ × 40″ finished size) you'll need:
- Fabric, 45″ width
    Color A, for blocks   = ⅝ yard
    Color B, for blocks, 4″ borders, and back   = 2½ yards
- Filling
    1¼ yard of 45″ light or medium weight bonded polyester batting, or one package of crib size batting
- Thread
    Choose a neutral color or match the color of one of your fabrics, providing it's not so much darker or lighter that it will show through.

TO MAKE YOUR PATCHWORK QUILT

1. Before you begin measuring your blocks, tear one end of your fabric from selvage to selvage about 2″ from the end of the piece to find the "straight" grain of the fabric. You'll need to snip through one selvage before tearing.

After you've found the "straight" of your fabric, measure and cut a 6″ strip across the width (from selvage to selvage). Cut the selvage off each end of the strip. Make a copy of the 6″ square template we've included with this design.

Using your template, divide each 6″ by 45″ strip into 6″ blocks, mark, and cut. You need eighteen 6″ blocks of each color, A and B, thirty-six blocks in all.

On the *wrong* side of each block, use a ruler and pencil to lightly draw a stitching line ¼″ in from all four sides of each block. (See Diagram 3.)

2. To assemble: Begin by laying your blocks on a table according to the design you planned on the graph paper. Use masking tape to number the front of fabric blocks (temporarily) according to your chart.

3. Lay block #1 on the table. Lay block #2 on top of block #1, right sides facing each other. Pin block #1 to block #2 according to Diagram 4 and sew together.

Make sure pins are perpendicular to seam line and no more than 1″ apart. This will allow the presser foot to glide right over the pins as you stitch.

Inspect the seam on both sides, making sure the right edge of square #1 is evenly attached to the left edge of square #2. Redo if necessary. This is the beginning of row 1. As you move along the row, be sure your previously stitched blocks are facing the same direction. The one you'll sew next will always go face down, and the next seam will always be on the right edge.

Continue sewing each square onto the one beside it until you've completed row 1 including blocks #1–#6. Use masking tape to mark this as row 1, and put it aside.

4. Now begin row 2 by flipping block #8 face down onto block #7, making sure you pin the blocks along the right edge. Be sure the blocks are facing the correct direction before you sew.

Continue attaching blocks until you have completed six rows. Press the wrong side of each row so that all seams in that row fold in one direction, alternating directions with each row. Follow Diagram 5. Lay all six rows face up on the table according to your plan.

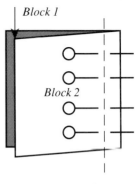

Diagram 4

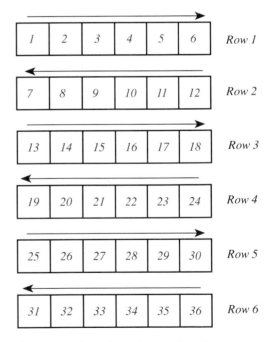

Press seams in each row in direction of arrows

Diagram 5

Traditional Patchwork Template
6" Template

5. Pick up row 2 and flip it up (right side down) onto row 1. Pin carefully every 1″, matching the seams between the blocks, and sew the rows together.

Continue pinning and sewing rows together until all six rows are attached. Be sure to check your plan between each row. Press seams so they lay flat, all toward the bottom of the quilt. You are now ready to add the borders, which you'll cut from color B.

Go to the section on Adding Borders on page 30.

Once the border is attached to the quilt face, proceed to assemble and quilt your quilt, following Steps 1 through 8 in the Basic Steps, page 33.

BLOCKS AND LATTICES QUILT

The blocks and lattices quilt is a good choice for a group project, because each person can design and make one or more blocks. You will need at least three or four colors of fabric for this design.

Draw a plan for your quilt on graph paper so you can visualize how it will look. Color the lattices, borders, and small intersection blocks in different colors to try out your design. Modify your plan until you're satisfied with the color combination you've chosen. You'll refer to this plan throughout the quiltmaking process.

Each block can be decorated with fabric crayons or fabric paint, appliqued, or embroidered. Or you may choose fabric already printed with a design for each block. Whichever design you choose, begin by creating a plan. Choose your fabric, mark, and cut the pieces. Wait until your quilt top is assembled before you cut the borders and the backing.

These measurements are for a finished quilt that will be approximately 38″ by 50″, assuming you make standard ¼″ quilt seams. All quilts are slightly different sizes because of varied seam allowances and designs.

MATERIALS
- Fabric, 45″ wide
  Color A, Blocks = 1½ yard
  Choose white or light-colored cotton or unbleached muslin, which you will decorate.
  Color B, Lattices and Borders = 1⅛ yard

Joann, "The B Quilt"
Northwood, New Hampshire

BLOCKS AND LATTICES QUILT

Choose a contrasting color you think will appeal to a small child. If you decide to make the border and the lattices from different colors, make sure they work well together. You will need ½ yard of color B for the lattices, the other ⅝ yard is for the borders.

Color C, Intersection Blocks = ¼ yard

You can use a scrap of fabric, either a print or solid, that looks nice with the lattice and border fabric.

Color D, Back = 1½ yard

Choose a contrasting color or the same color as B.

◆ Filling = 1½ yard of 45″ light or medium weight bonded polyester batting

◆ Thread

Choose a neutral color that maches your blocks.

Begin with fabric color A. If you plan to decorate the blocks with crayons or fabric markers, use whatever fabric is recommended by the manufacturer. Remember to wash, dry, and press *all* your fabric before you begin.

Find the straight grain of the fabric (see page 17 in Patchwork Quilt). Cut off both selvages. Using graph paper make a 9″ square template. Use your template to mark and cut twelve 9″ blocks.

Prepare these twelve blocks with your chosen design method. See the quilt pictured here for design ideas. Your design can be painted on the square with special fabric paint. It can be drawn with Pentel Fabric Crayons or Niji Fabricolor markers or appliqued or embroidered with an original design. (Unless you're very experienced, get some expert help to applique or embroider.)

You'll have the best luck if you draw the design for each block on paper first, then transfer it to fabric. Use whatever method is recommended by the marker manufacturer to make your image permanent. Make sure the paints or markers are non-toxic.

Important Note: Remember to leave ½″ on all sides around the block with no design for space and seam allowances.

Avoid any paints, markers, or methods that result in rough or scratchy surfaces. Think of the surface a baby snuggling up to your square would like. Sign your square with your first name using a permanent fabric marker, or embroider it.

*D.V.B.S., The First Presbyterian Church
Willow Grove, Pennsylvania*

*St. John Episcopal Church,
6th, 7th, 8th Grade Sunday School
Olney, Maryland*

Marking the Lattice
Diagram 6

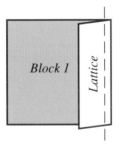

Diagram 7

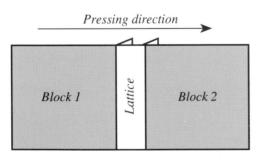

Diagram 8

Lay out twelve blocks in a pleasing design, and use tape to temporarily number each block 1 through 12. On graph paper, draw your final plan, which you'll refer to as you assemble your quilt.

Next, you'll cut the lattices and borders.

Work with the contrasting fabric for lattices and borders. (Or use two colors here, one for lattices, another color for borders.) Wash, dry, and press the contrasting color.

For the lattices, you'll need ½ yard 45″ wide. Remove selvage and measure across the width. Use a yardstick and pencil to mark five 3″ by 45″ strips on the wrong side of fabric. Then cut the strips. Using the template copied from this book, mark and cut seventeen 9″ by 3″ pieces.

Use a ruler and pencil to mark a ¼″ seam allowance (on the wrong side of the fabric) around the edges of each lattice strip. (See Diagram 6.) Set them aside.

Next, you'll work on the small intersection squares, using color C. This ¼ yard should be washed, dried, and pressed. Then, find the straight grain. Use the template copied from this book to mark and cut six 3″-square intersection blocks. With a ruler and pencil, mark ¼″ seam allowances around the edges on the wrong side of each 3″ square.

ASSEMBLING THE FACE

1. Lay block #1 face up on the table. Lay a lattice strip face down on the right edge of block #1. Pin the two together so that pins lie perpendicular to the seam line. Sew the lattice strip to the right side of block #1. Open the lattice strip so that both pieces are face up. (See Diagram 7.)

2. Lay block #2 face down along right edge of the lattice strip. Pin and sew along marked ¼″ seam allowance. Open your piece and turn face up. You have two blocks connected by one lattice strip. Make sure your blocks are facing the same direction. (See Diagram 8.)

3. Lay another lattice strip along the right edge of block #2, right sides of fabric facing together. Pin together and sew along the marked seam, sewing the lattice strip to the right side of block #2. Open the lattice strip so that all pieces are face up.

4. Lay block #3 face down along right edge of the second lattice strip. Pin and sew. Open your piece and turn face up. You now have three blocks connected by two lattice strips. This is one block/lattice row. Make sure your blocks are all facing in the same direction. Complete all four of these block/lattice rows. (See Diagram 9.)

5. Next, you'll work with the small intersection squares and the remaining lattice strips to make the lattice/intersection rows. Lay a lattice strip horizontally, face up on the table in front of you. Lay a 3″ intersection square face down on the right end of the strip, matching the edges.

Pin together and stitch along marked seams. Open strip face up so that square is on right, lattice strip on left. Lay another lattice strip horizontally face down, matching right edge of square. Pin and sew. Open strip face up and continue until you have three lattices alternating with two intersection squares. (See Diagram 10.) Set this row aside.

Repeat for three lattice/intersection rows.

6. The final step is to join the block/lattice rows and the lattice/intersection rows. To begin this step, press completed block/lattice rows and lattice/intersection rows. Press the seams in alternating directions, according to Diagrams 9 and 10. A steam iron works best to keep seams flat.

7. Align the first block/lattice row with a strip of lattice/intersection, face to face. Match seams carefully and accurately, pin at right angles to seam line, and stitch. Open the seam to check intersection joinings for accuracy. Redo if necessary to make your seams accurate and even. When done correctly, intersection squares will perfectly match vertical lattice strip seams. Make any adjustments at this point. See Diagram 11.

8. Continue to add block/lattice rows alternately with lattice/intersection rows until this part of the top is complete. Refer to your design plan and to diagrams for assistance as needed.

Finish your quilt face by adding the border strips. Refer to section on Adding Borders on page 30 to make the border. Then proceed with Steps 1 through 8 from The Basic Eight Steps on page 33.

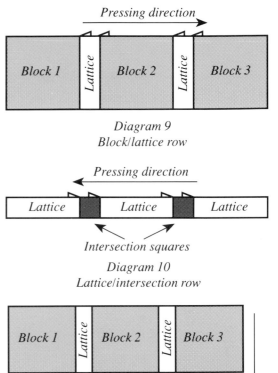

Diagram 9
Block/lattice row

Diagram 10
Lattice/intersection row

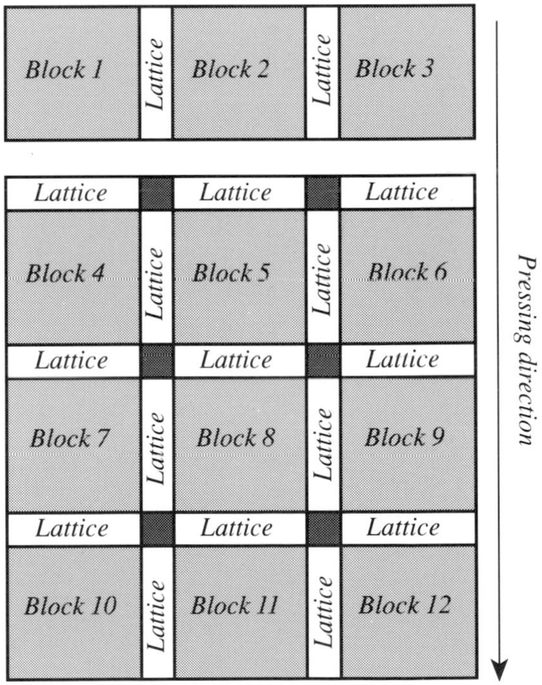

Diagram 11

3" x 9" Template for Lattice

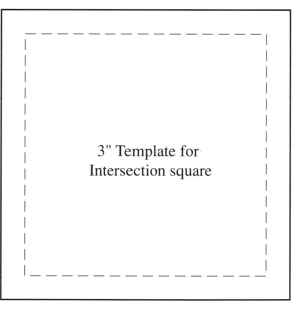

3" Template for
Intersection square

THE CREATIVE STYLE QUILT

In this book, the creative style means that any design, such as teddy bears, rabbits, hearts, balloons, or any other figure can be embroidered, painted, drawn, or appliqued, and applied to the quilt top to create your desired effect. You can combine designs or get some ideas from other quilters or pictures in this book. Choose one or more techniques as the spirit moves you! The designs you can create are limited only by your imagination and your experience in sewing or completing them.

The quilt shown here with directions uses a machine applique technique and measures approximately 40″ square.

MATERIALS

◆ Fabric, 100% cotton, 45″ wide
  Color A, for blocks and hearts   = 1¼ yards
  Color B, for blocks, centerpiece heart, and cornerstones   = ¾ yard
  Color C, for borders, centerpiece block, and back   = 2¼ yards
◆ Filling = 1½ yard of 45″ bonded polyester batting
◆ Thread, neutral color that maches your blocks

First, draw your quilt to scale on graph paper. Color your plan according to the fabric you've selected. (See Diagram 12.)

Your blocks will be 12″ square before sewing.

Four of the color B blocks are appliqued with hearts made from color A, and the centerpiece color C block is appliqued with two hearts made from colors A and B. Of course, you can design any combination that pleases you. Be sure to wash, dry, and press your fabric before beginning.

Make a 12″ square template. Use it to cut four 12″ color A blocks, four 12″ color B blocks, and one color C block.

Trace the heart templates we've included. Using your templates and a pencil, draw eight 9″ hearts and two 7″ hearts (for the centerpiece) onto the wrong side of color A. Cut two 9″ hearts from color B, also for the centerpiece.

Lay a 9″ color A heart face up on the table. Lay another 9″ color A heart face down on it and pin all the way around the edges, pins pointing toward the center.

Diagram 12

Ruby
Lexington, Massachusetts

CREATIVE STYLE QUILT

Sew a ¼ inch seam all the way around. Trim close to the stitching line, especially at the points of the heart.

Pull the layers apart so you can make an approximately 2″ slit in the center of one heart only. Turn inside out through the slit so the seams are on the inside. (See Diagram 13.) Press. Now you have a nice finished edge to applique onto each color B block and the centerpiece. Repeat for all six hearts. Now you are ready to applique the hearts to your squares. You might want to stuff the hearts with a little batting to make them puff out a little, or maybe you'll stuff only the centerpiece heart.

To applique the hearts, begin by pinning the four 9″ color A hearts in place, slit side down, in the center of the four color B blocks. Baste close to the edge of the hearts. Then hand stitch each heart in place using close, small stitches. Or use embroidery stitches or machine stitch using a close zig-zag stitch. For the centerpiece hearts, first applique the larger color C heart in place, and then applique the smaller color A heart in the center of the color C heart.

To embroider words, plan your words on graph paper first. Then, with a pencil, lightly outline the words in place on the centerpiece block color B, or on the heart that will become the center of the quilt. Using a hoop, embroider your design in colors that will complement colors A, B, and C. Embroidery should be done before you applique the heart onto the quilt. If you embroider onto the quilt face, complete the embroidery before you attach the filling and back.

To paint, if you choose to use fabric paint, plan your design first on graph paper. Then transfer your design to the centerpiece block. Using special textile or fabric paints, complete your design following the directions on the paint you select.

Make sure the paints you select are non-toxic, washable, and don't leave rough areas on the quilt. It's a good idea to try out the paint you've selected on a scrap of fabric before you use it on your quilt. Create a surface that a baby would like to snuggle up to.

Now that you've completed the applique and embroidery on the blocks, lay them out on a table according to your plan.

Lay block 2 face down onto block 1 (face up), pin the right edge, and sew. Open your work, checking to be sure blocks are in proper position. Lay block 3 face

Diagram 13
Sewing heart together and
cutting slit to turn right side out

down onto block 2, pin the right edge, and sew. Open row 1 and check to be sure all blocks are upright. Put aside row 1. Repeat instructions for rows 2 and 3. Press seams to the left and to the right on alternating rows.

When you have assembled each row, attach the three rows. (Refer to Step 2 on page 17 of Traditional Patchwork design for more detailed instructions.) Then go to the section on Adding Borders, page 30. After you've added your borders, go to steps 1 through 8 of The Basic Eight Steps (page 33) to finish your quilt.

You can make a large variety of quilts using these basic nine blocks and adding your own applique shapes and designs. Different color combinations will create entirely different effects. Go wild! Be creative.

Main St. School
Exeter, New Hampshire

Riverside Junior High School
7th and 8th Grade
Springfield, Vermont

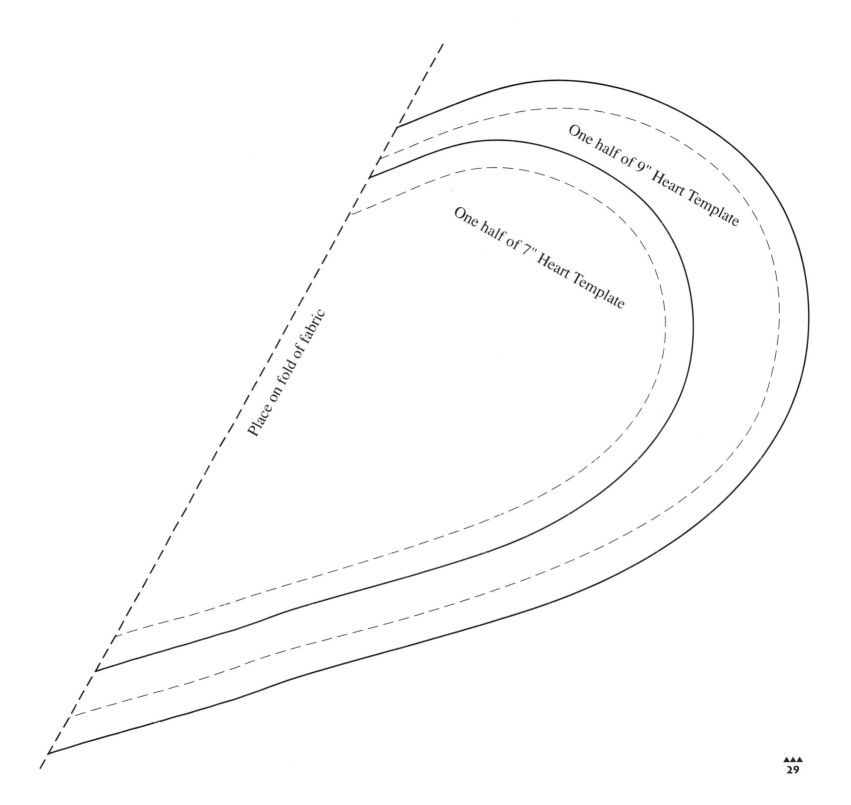

One half of 9" Heart Template

One half of 7" Heart Template

Place on fold of fabric

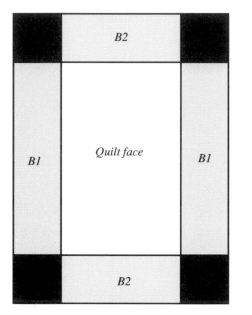

Diagram 14

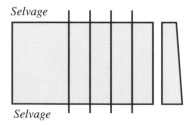

Selvage

Selvage

Diagram 15
Cutting borders

Chapter 3
ADDING BORDERS

Most quilt tops look better with one or more borders. If you follow these directions, step by step, you'll find that borders are relatively easy to complete. They give a nice professional finish to your quilt with a minimum of effort.

Borders are the last element added to the quilt face. Refer to your original graph paper plan. We show a 4″ border with 4″ cornerstones on the traditional patchwork quilt, the block and lattice quilt, and on the creative style quilt. (See Diagram 14.)

Borders are made from fabric that has been cut from selvage to selvage, as shown in Diagram 15.

Buy a little extra yardage because the first strip you tear to find the "straight" of the fabric, may not be uniform. All strips will be 45″ long because you will cut them across the width of 45″ fabric. You'll need four 4″ by 45″ strips, so buy ⅝ yard of fabric. You'll also need a piece of contrasting color fabric, about 12″ by 12″ square (to be on the safe side), for the corners.

HOW TO CUT BORDERS

1. Snip the edge of selvage about 1″ to 2″ from end. Then tear fabric from one selvage to the other in order to find the "straight" of the fabric. When fabric is cut it may look straight, but it's usually not cut along the weave, or the "straight" of the fabric. You may need to try this tearing technique several times if the cut is extremely crooked.

2. Once you have a straight edge that has been torn all the way across, measure four strips of 4″ each. Cut the four 4″ strips all the way across to the other edge, giving you four 4″ by 45″ strips.

ATTACHING THE BORDERS

Lay your quilt face on the table and smooth it out with your hands.

1. Measure the two long (vertical) sides of your quilt face. Are they different? If the sides are not the same length, add the two measurements together, and divide by two to find the average length. Using this average length, cut two vertical border strips. Use masking tape to mark a small "B1" on the *wrong* side of each vertical border strip.

2. Measure short (horizontal) sides of your quilt face. If the sides aren't the same length, add the two measurements together, and divide by two to find the average. Use this average length to measure and cut your two horizontal border strips. Use masking tape to mark a small "B2" on the *wrong* side of each horizontal border strip.

3. Do the vertical sides first. Use pins to mark the midpoint of each "B1" border strip. Use pins to mark the midpoint of the vertical edges of the quilt face.

4. With the quilt face right side up, lay one "B1" border wrong side up along the edge of the face. Match midpoint pin marks and pin in place. Pin "B1" border to vertical quilt side at the ends. (See Diagram 16.) Continue pinning every 1″, easing any fullness evenly across the edge. Make sure pins are perpendicular to seam line. Sew a ¼″ seam. Repeat this process for the other vertical side. Press the seams to the left. Open quilt face in front of you, vertical borders in place. (See Diagram 17.)

5. Now you add the cornerstones. We recommend using cornerstones with your borders. They give your quilt a nice professional look, and help to keep the quilt square. Refer to your quilt plan. You'll need four 4″ squares of a contrasting fabric for the cornerstones. Measure and cut a 4″ strip from your cornerstone fabric. Using a 4″ template copied from this book, cut four 4″ square cornerstones.

6. Lay one of the "B2" border strips on the table right side up. Lay a cornerstone, wrong side up, on each end of the "B2" strip. Pin and stitch ¼″ seams to join cornerstones to each end of the "B2" strip. Press the seams in alternate directions according to Diagrams 17 and 18.

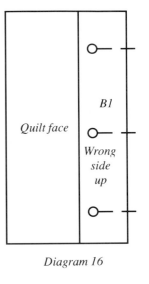

Diagram 16

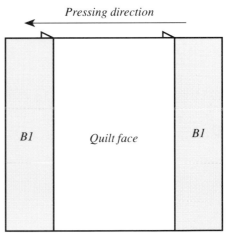

Diagram 17

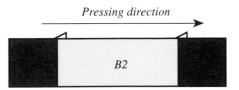

Diagram 18

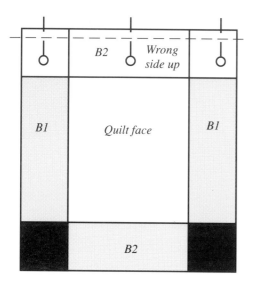

Diagram 19

Repeat for other "B2" horizontal border.

7. Attaching horizontal ("B2") borders. Lay quilt face right side up on table. Lay "B2" borders (with cornerstones attached) wrong side up, one on each end of the quilt. Match midpoint pin marks and pin in place at midpoint. (See Diagram 19.)

Carefully match seamline of cornerstones with seamline of vertical borders and pin in place. Ease any fullness evenly as you pin the rest of the seam in place every 1″. Make sure pins are perpendicular to seam line. Sew a ¼″ seam. Open quilt face in front of you. The quilt face is done. Isn't it beautiful!

To assemble your quilt, please refer to The Basic Eight Steps described on page 33.

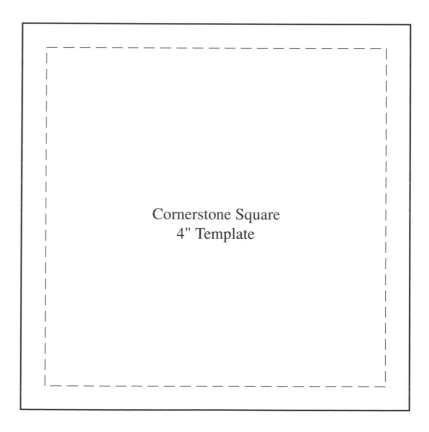

Cornerstone Square
4″ Template

Chapter 4
HOW TO MAKE AN ABC QUILT

THE BASIC EIGHT STEPS

These eight steps will help you finish your quilt. When you have completed your quilt face according to the directions, you are ready to assemble your quilt.

CUTTING THE FABRIC

1. Once the quilt face is completed, measure each side, trimming any excess to make it even. Then measure so that the back is 1″ bigger than the quilt face all around. Cut the backing fabric and the filling to the size of your completed quilt face plus a 1″ margin all the way around. (The best finished size is approximately 36″ wide by 44″ long, but don't cut your quilt face.) The size of your quilt back will depend on which design you choose.

ASSEMBLING THE LAYERS

2. Lay backing fabric right side up on table. Center the quilt face, right side down, on backing fabric. Smooth out and pin from the middle of each side to the corners. (See Diagram 20.) Place the pins about 1″ apart all the way around the quilt with the point of the pins pointing in toward the center.

To stitch: Set the stitch length on the sewing machine for 12 to 15 stitches per inch. Start stitching in the middle of the bottom edge, leaving a ½″ seam around the edges. Stop stitching ½″ before you reach the corner. With the needle still in the fabric, lift the presser foot and pivot 90 degrees around the corner.

Lower the presser foot and continue stitching the next side to within ½″ of the

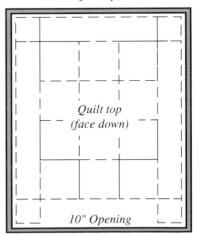

Quilt back (face up)

Quilt top (face down)

10″ Opening

Diagram 20

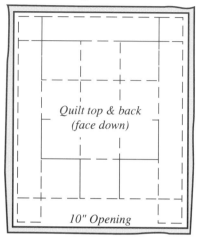

Batting underneath

Quilt top & back (face down)

10" Opening

Diagram 21

Diagram 22
Blind stitch opening

next corner and pivot again, continuing this process until you reach the side where you began. Leave a 10″ opening in the middle of the side where you started. Lockstitch in the last few stitches by reversing and sewing back over them. Remove the quilt from the machine. Remove the pins.

3. Trim the backing even with quilt top. Lay stitched quilt face and backing on top of batting, with seam side of quilt face on top. Pin in place with quilt pins, starting from center, and pinning every 2″. Trim batting approximately ¼″ larger than quilt face and back. (See Diagram 21.)

Switch to a #14 needle. Change machine stitch to 10 to 12 stitches per inch. With batting underneath, stitch along previous stitching line, beginning at the 10″ opening, pivoting at corners. When you come back around to the opening, lift the top layer, and stitch only the backing and batting together. Back stitch to lock the stitching. Remove pins.

A Tip: If your filling keeps catching on the machine, pin thin strips of tissue paper to the filling stitching line. Keeping the tissue on the bottom, sew through the quilt layers and tissue paper. Rip away the paper after removing the quilt from the machine.

4. Trim the edge of the filling and the fabric to ¼″ total seam allowance. Diagonally cut away the corners close to the stitching line.

5. Turn the quilt right side out through the opening by reaching in and grasping the opposite corners. The filling will be sandwiched in between the face and back. Reach inside the opening and push out each corner to make nice points on the corners. Press the quilt lightly at the seams, turning in the raw edges of the opening. Stitch the opening shut, using small, tight hand stitches. (See Diagram 22.)

QUILTING

6. Before you begin quilting, baste around the outside edges approximately ½″ in from the edge. Then using long stitches, baste all layers together in parallel rows of basting 6″ apart. This basting will prevent shifting of layers as you machine or hand quilt.

First, machine or hand stitch through all the layers 1″ or 2″ from the edge, depending on your design. Then you can machine or hand stitch through all the layers outlining certain motifs in the design of the fabric. Or create your own design with stitches, making sure you stitch all the layers firmly together at least every 6″.

For machine quilting, set the stitches at 6 to 8 stitches per inch. Topstitch through all the layers, backstitching at the beginning and end of the stitching. You may want to "stitch in the ditch," which means to stitch the layers together following seam lines made when you attached your blocks, lattices, and borders. (See Diagram 23.)

For hand quilting, use small stitches to outline designs, or create subtle designs with the stitches themselves. Make sure the layers are held together at least every 6″ all over the quilt.

Instead of hand quilting, you may wish to hand tie your quilt. (See photo, page 26.) For hand tying, first measure and mark your quilt (with a washable or disappearing marker). For an all over design, measure approximately every 4″ in each direction from the center, where you'll put a tie. For other designs, choose places for ties that will enhance your design, such as intersections of blocks and lattices, centers of flowers, etc. Be sure that the quilt is tied at least every 4″ to 6″ for sturdiness.

Once you have planned and marked positions for ties, thread a needle with 2 strands of crochet cotton, or 6 strands of embroidery floss. Starting at the center of the quilt and working toward the edges, insert the needle from the front, across ⅛″ on the back, and up to the front again. Tie a surgeon's knot and cut ends to 1″. (See surgeon's knot Diagram 24.)

FINISHING

7. Autograph the lower right corner of your quilt with "ABC Quilts, Love and Comfort to You, and your first name and state." Use a laundry pen or permanent fabric marker. (Do not use a regular magic marker.) Even better, embroider your name for a special symbol of love. Please do not use the word AIDS on any quilt.

8. Then make sure your quilt is "baby-ready." Baby ready means that you've carefully checked your quilt to make sure there are no hidden or stray pins and no threads longer than 1″ anywhere on your quilt. You are now ready to send your quilt to ABC Quilts. For information, send a #10 stamped, self-addressed envelope to PO Box 107, Weatherford, OK, 73096.

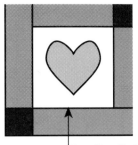

Seamline ditch

Diagram 23

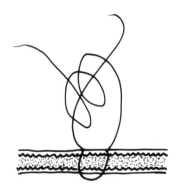

Right over left. Wrap twice. Pull tight.

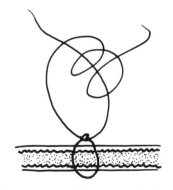

Left over right. Wrap twice. Pull tight.

Diagram 24
Surgeon's knot

DEAR PARENTS, TEACHERS, YOUTH LEADERS, AND OTHERS,

We're pleased that you and your children have decided to help ABC Quilts by making a quilt to provide love and comfort to a baby born HIV-positive, or with drug- or alcohol-related problems. We've had many requests for information from parents, teachers, youth leaders, and others who work with kids who would like to include both making the quilts and ABC Quilt Talk in their projects. Talking with kids about AIDS, drug and alcohol awareness, and family and sex education isn't always easy.

Many adults feel that they don't want to give kids any ideas about sex or drugs or alcohol abuse because they're too young, or what they don't know can't hurt them. Usually, however, kids have heard more from their friends than their parents or other adults in their lives could imagine, much of it downright wrong. And because of all the media coverage kids are exposed to, most kids have a great deal of anxiety about AIDS and sex, drugs and alcohol.

In conversation with my grandchildren, neighbors, friends, family, and the media, I hear confusion, concern, fear, and false concepts. A high school student said to me, "I don't understand how a baby could get AIDS." A four-year-old said, "If you have sex, you die." I asked her what sex means, and she said, "hugging and kissing." A middle school child wants to know how a baby could catch AIDS from his mother. Talk about fear and anxiety.

Yes, talk. Talking is the best way to figure out what everyone knows and how they feel about what they know. The Facts and Discussion Starter resource section in this book is designed to help kids and adults talk to each other about difficult topics. You can use the information in this book and the opportunity provided by making a quilt together to discover how the kids feel. You can also discover what they think you feel, and share with them how you do. We often have misperceptions about how others feel about controversial statements. And your kids may not know exactly how you feel.

Our children hear mixed messages from all directions about both AIDS and drugs. Our task is to determine just what they know and understand and what is age-appropriate information for them. As parents, teachers, and grandparents, too, we have a huge job to teach our children and young people that there are ways that can guarantee their safety and the chance to live a long, healthy, and worthwhile life. What a challenge!

Quiltmaking seems to be an excellent medium to encourage conversation and discussion. The Japanese call it "talking through quilting," which was embroidered in Japanese on one of the quilts that they sent to us.

Quilting bees have been called our first group therapy sessions. They still work that way. Adults have reported to me that making quilts for HIV-infected babies creates such a warm, friendly, therapeutic environment, that the children feel comfortable asking questions and sharing their sometimes vast but incorrect knowledge about these epidemics.

We have included in this book bits and pieces of information, as fact vs. myth, and questions and answers about AIDS and substance abuse. These are intended to stimulate discussions and to help resolve anxieties. Our information is by no means comprehensive. It is not intended to substitute for the many books, pamphlets, and other publications available on the complex topics of substance abuse and AIDS. We have suggested a few sources that have been recommended to us. There are many others. Many sources provide information at nominal costs or at no cost. We'd like to hear your suggestions of good materials, which we will pass on to others.

ABC Quilts have been called the baby's best friend, a constant source of love and comfort, available to them at all times. The children respond to this image and really have a great time working together on a common goal. This cooperative effort is also a lot of fun! Starting with choosing the design, fabrics, colors, shapes, and then making a plan to follow, children learn to measure, use graph paper to enlarge designs, and use the sewing machine. What a sense of accomplishment they feel when it all evolves into a cozy little comforter.

The quilting directions are all quite simple and can be accomplished by elementary or middle school age children with some help from parents, teachers, or more experienced quilters from the community. Everyone has a need to help in some way, and many people are just waiting to be asked.

We hope that by encouraging young people to participate in healthy activities that develop self-esteem and by improving communication with them through quilt talk, that we can affect their decision-making process when they confront issues concerning AIDS, alcohol, and drugs.

Last, but certainly not least, ABC Quiltmaking develops many valuable motor and cognitive skills, as well as altruism and social consciousness. Children feel empowered when they can make a difference in the life of another child. Many thanks to you all.

Love and comfort to you,
Ellen Ahlgren and the ABC Quilts Volunteers

This information is only a starting point for discussions about perceptions and attitudes about AIDS and alcohol and other drugs. Use the following information in your own words and as appropriate for the age level of your group. This is not a comprehensive curriculum. Please use the resource section at the end of this section. It will point you in some directions to help you find more publications and films and videos on the subjects that interest you.

FACTS AND DISCUSSION STARTERS ABOUT AIDS AND SUBSTANCE ABUSE

Did You Know?

AIDS is short for Acquired Immune Deficiency Syndrome, a disease that breaks down the immune system. It leaves the body defenseless against a variety of infections and cancers. AIDS is caused by a virus called HIV, which is short for Human Immunodeficiency Virus. A person can have HIV and not have AIDS. There is no known cure for AIDS at this time.

Did you know you cannot get AIDS from:

sneezing, hugging,
sharing eating utensils, drinking glasses, or cups,
shots at the doctor's office,
giving blood,
mosquitos, dogs, cats, canaries,
toilet seats, books, doorknobs,
sharing towels, combs,
playing together?

Why do people call drug abuse and HIV "allied epidemics"?

Using drugs or alcohol impairs your ability to make good judgments. Many drug users and alcohol users forget their good judgment and engage in dangerous behaviors while "under the influence," which puts them at risk of infection by HIV and other sexually transmitted diseases (STD's). All STD's endanger your health, but HIV is even worse—it endangers your life.

How do babies get AIDS?

Babies get AIDS from their HIV-infected mothers, either before or during childbirth or from breastfeeding. Babies born to an HIV-infected mother have a 30% to 50% chance of being infected. Researchers don't know why some babies develop AIDS and others don't. Babies who contract AIDS at birth may live up to five or ten years.

How do the mothers get AIDS?

Women get AIDS from
◆ having sex with an HIV-infected man without using a new latex condom every time.
◆ sharing needles or "works" to inject drugs.
◆ receiving transfusions or blood products before July 1985.

How do I know I didn't get AIDS from my mother?

If you had been infected with HIV during your mother's pregnancy, you would likely be quite sick from AIDS by now and so would your mother.

What's the "window" period?

The HIV antibody blood test is the only way to know for sure whether a person has been infected by the AIDS virus. The "window" period is the time between when a person is infected and when the antibodies or "fighter cells" are detectable by testing. During the window period a person can transmit HIV.

FACTS AND MYTHS ABOUT HIV AND AIDS

You can tell if someone shoots drugs or has HIV or AIDS.

Myth—The fact is you can't assume someone hasn't experimented with drugs or been exposed to HIV just because he or she looks a certain way. You can't recognize HIV infection by looking at someone, because most people who are infected by HIV don't even know it themselves. It can take as many as seven to ten years for visible symptoms to appear.

I would know if one of my friends had AIDS.

Myth—Because of the stigma and social rejection involved, friends may not tell you even if they know they are HIV positive. The fact is, a blood test is the only way to tell for sure. A blood test looks for the antibodies, or the "fighter cells," that your body makes to fight infection by the AIDS virus. These antibodies are produced by an infected person's blood within a few weeks to six months of infection, or longer.

You can't have HIV and not know it.

Myth—The fact is most people infected with the HIV virus have no symptoms at all and feel and look perfectly healthy for a long time. It can take anywhere from a few months to as long as ten years for active AIDS symptoms to appear. A person who is HIV-infected can infect other people almost as soon as they are infected. Some of the nicest people have HIV and don't even know it because they got it from someone else who didn't know they had it either.

You can protect yourself against AIDS.

Fact—Total abstinence from drugs and sex is the only certain protection. The next best way to protect yourself is to avoid shooting drugs or having sex with someone who is infected. This sounds easier than it is. A blood test is the only sure way to know if someone is HIV-infected. Those infected don't necessarily know it. Just "knowing" someone for a long time doesn't protect you. Love doesn't protect you. Being nice, or pretty, or handsome, or well built doesn't protect you.

I practice safe sex, so I definitely won't get AIDS.

Myth—The fact is that the term is "safer" sex. Safe sex means you are in a mutually monogamous relationship with someone who is definitely not infected. Otherwise, condoms with spermicide are safer than no protection, but they are not always effective.

AIDS can't happen to me, I'm too young. Only gays and druggies get AIDS.

Myth—The fact is that it's risky behaviors that put you at risk—not age, background, race, gender, or sexual orientation. As of early 1989 more than 18,000 Americans between the ages of 20 and 29 have been diagnosed with AIDS. These numbers increase every year. Since it can take as long as ten years for symptoms to appear, *most of these people became infected when they were teenagers.*

I've already said yes to some risky encounters, so I might as well just keep on enjoying myself, I'm probably doomed anyway.

Myth—Just because you've said yes before, doesn't mean you have to keep on saying yes. Saying no might not be the popular thing to do, and at a moment of passion it can be really difficult. What you can do is think of some of the pressure tactics people have used on you in the past, and while you are clear-headed, rehearse what you'd like to answer. For instance, if someone says you have to do it to prove your love, you might answer, "Is it love if you have to prove it?" How will you feel about your decision next week? Next year?

If you are worried that you might have AIDS or another sexually transmitted disease, get some professional advice and testing. That's the only way to reassure yourself so you can stop worrying about your past behavior and get on with making good decisions for your life.

We're really in love and we've been going steady for over a year so we don't have to worry about practicing safer sex.

Myth—The reasons for a relationship to become a sexual one are complicated and important, and have little to do with how much in love you are or how long you have been going steady. Love and "knowing someone" have nothing to do with your risk for HIV exposure. Past and present behaviors of each partner are the only relevant factors. The number of previous sexual partners you've both had and the IV drug use of those and all their partners is what determines your risk. Sexual abstinence is the only guaranteed safe option. Next best is practicing safer sex—using a new latex condom with spermicide every time.

AGREE/DISAGREE DISCUSSION STARTERS

If I thought I was at risk of being HIV positive, I would talk to my parents.
Why or why not? Would your parents jump to conclusions if you brought up the subject of AIDS? Have you ever talked to them about sex and how they feel about it? What do they know about AIDS?

Knowing that a friend had AIDS wouldn't affect our friendship.

I would have a problem working on a team project with someone who has AIDS.

I would have a problem hugging a person who has AIDS.
How about sharing a bathroom?

Some questions to ask:
◆ How can you know for sure if someone else is HIV-positive when it takes as much as ten years for AIDS symptoms to appear?
◆ How can you find out if someone has engaged in some dangerous behaviors in the past when many people either don't know what's dangerous, they forgot, or they know but they won't honestly tell you?
◆ How can you convince your boyfriend or girlfriend that AIDS can happen to anyone, that love doesn't protect you from AIDS, and that you owe it to yourself and each other to protect yourself and those you care about?

FACTS AND MYTHS ABOUT DRUG ABUSE

It's much safer to chew tobacco than to smoke it.
Myth—It's true that you won't contract lung cancer or emphysema from chewing. However, the fact is that tobacco contains many harsh chemicals and drugs that can cause mouth cancer when chewed. Is one cancer better than another?

Alcohol is a leading cause of death in the U.S.
Fact—Half of all fatal highway crashes, 17–53% of falls, 38% of drownings, and 37–68% of fires and burns are alcohol-related. Two out of every five people in the U.S. will be in an alcohol related car crash in their lifetime.

Alcohol is the most widely abused drug in the United States.
Fact—Alcoholism and related problems cost the nation an estimated $85.8 billion in 1988, $27.5 billion more than illicit use of other drugs. Do you know for certain how many of your friends drink? How many abstain from all drugs including alcohol?

Anyone who doesn't drink is out of it.
Myth—The fact is some of the most important learning young people complete in the teen years has to do with forming good relationships with others. True friends appreciate you for who you are, not what you do or don't do. If you feel good about what you're doing, you don't need others to do it too just to make you feel okay.
Fact—Twenty-five percent of high school students are abstainers.

Just because I use alcohol or other drugs occasionally, doesn't mean I'll become an alcoholic or drug addict.
Myth—The fact is no one starts using alcohol or drugs intending to become addicted. No one thinks, "I want to be an alcoholic or a drug addict when I grow up." Kids begin to experiment because alcohol and other drugs provide a temporary escape from problems. They like the feeling. When the "high" is over, the problems are still there. They don't want to deal with the problems they originally tried to escape, so they do some more alcohol or other drugs. Down, up, down, up. Pretty soon, their bodies can't stand to be down anymore and need to stay high all the time just to "feel normal." Their

body begins to crave the "high." Then the high becomes more important than anything else. It begins to rule their life. Drug addicts and alcoholics need help escaping their "ruler." You can't make others stop, but you can take care of yourself and talk about your feelings in situations where others are pressuring you.

It's okay to use steroids for a few months in order to make the team.

Myth—The fact is that steroids are a powerful class of drugs with dangerous side effects. In the short term, steroids provide a jolt of aggressiveness that sometimes causes erratic or psychotic or suicidal behavior. Athletes often refer to this as "roid rage." Prolonged use of steroids has caused sterility, kidney failure, cancer, heart disease, and other diseases. Even short term use of steroids can cause hair loss and severe acne. Sharing needles to inject steroids puts you at risk of infection with HIV and AIDS, which are fatal.

An alcohol-related family problem affects one in four American families.

Fact—Alcohol affects far more than the person who drinks. Alcoholics tend to emotionally, and sometimes physically, abuse their families and loved ones. Alcoholics will spend all their time, energy, and money to support their habit—at the expense of not meeting the needs of their families. People who grow up in alcoholic families are more likely to become alcoholic and/or addicted to other things. Plus they often carry the dysfunctional ways of relating to others into their own families and relationships.

Using alcohol on weekends or special occasions is okay.

Myth—The fact is that at least 3.3 million drinking teenagers are showing signs that may lead to the development of alcoholism. Do you know what those signs are? Do you know what is considered "moderate" versus "heavy" drinking?

You can stop a parent or friend from abusing alcohol or other drugs.

Myth—It's important to remember that kids or adults can't control, can't cure, and didn't cause someone else's substance abuse. What kids can do is communicate their feelings to a trusted person and take care of themselves. The only person's behavior you can control or change is your own.

AGREE/DISAGREE DISCUSSION STARTERS

Drinking makes you more popular.
The questions here must be more popular with whom, and why?

The only people who really influence a kid's decision about whether or not to do drugs is their friends.
Whose opinion makes a difference? Where does your most valued information come from, and why? What is the most difficult situation to resist? How do you feel when you know that someone you care about engages in risky behavior?

Smoking is no big deal when you consider all the other "dangerous" drugs.
Check the statistics on how many deaths and medical costs are directly associated with tobacco. Do you know which diseases have been proven to be directly caused by smoking? Why do you think people have such a hard time quitting smoking? What is your state's position on smoking in public places? How do you feel about those rules? What about "secondary" or indirect smoking?

All TV beer commercials should be banned by federal law.
In 1989 the alcoholic beverage industry spent $1.2 billion on advertising, more than was spent by the household equipment and electronic entertainment industries combined. Three of the top twenty-five spot television advertisers produce beer.

A celebration is better with champagne.
What is the part of a celebration that's most important? What is the feeling we're trying to attain?

There are no good reasons for using drugs.
How about prescription drugs? Is it okay to use other people's prescriptions?

RESOURCES

There are lots of books, brochures, and videos available about AIDS and drugs and how they relate to children and teenagers. Please inform yourself and everyone you know as completely as possible and spread the word. It could be a matter of life and death for someone.

For more information on AIDS call or write the following places:

◆ The Department of Public Health in your state has information available.

◆ Local hospitals are excellent sources of information.

◆ The American Red Cross has lots of publications and some videos you can borrow free of charge.

◆ Check your library, talk to your teachers, your school nurse, your parents, your minister, priest, or rabbi.

◆ The Elisabeth Kübler-Ross Center has many interesting books and audiotapes on the topic of pediatric AIDS. Two books with a lot of information are *AIDS, You Can't Catch It Holding Hands* by Niki de Saint Phalle ($6.95, Lapis Press), and *Children and the AIDS Virus* by Rosmarie Hausherr ($4.95, Clarion, Houghton Mifflin). You can order them and others from the publishers or from: EKR Center, South Rte. 616, Headwaters, VA 24442.

◆ Ask your library about *Rodale's Straight Talk*, an excellent quarterly magazine for teens about AIDS and drugs and other teen issues. Or order it from Rodale Books, 33 East Minor Street, Emmaus, PA 18098, telephone (215) 967-8660.

For more information on alcohol and other drugs call or write the following places:

◆ NCADD, the National Council on Alcoholism and Drug Dependence, telephone (800) 475-HOPE, and ask about their publications, referrals, and prevention programs.

◆ Your state Department of Public Health. Most have substance abuse agencies that have free information, curricula, and sometimes visiting speakers.

◆ The Scott Newman Center in Los Angeles, telephone (800) 783-6396. They have lots of neat projects to help kids stay drug free. They also provide teaching materials, lesson plans, and resources for teaching programs to help children to resist drug/alcohol advertising by creating a television commercial of their own.

◆ Read *The Broken Cord*, by Michael Dorris, (HarperCollins Publishers, 1989) a story of a child born with fetal alcohol syndrome and what his adopted father did about it and felt about it.

◆ You may not have a problem with drugs or alcohol, but maybe you know someone who does. Call a local Alcoholics Anonymous, AlAnon, or Alateen group (local telephone numbers are listed in your directory).

◆ Or call the National Institute of Drug Abuse hotline toll-free at 1-800-662-HELP for ideas on what to do.

When we encounter a painful situation in life, we all need comfort. A good way to find comfort is to reach out to another person. An ABC Quilt provides love and comfort to a little kid who really needs it. And making an ABC Quilt will comfort you too, by giving you a chance to give a touchable expression of your love. Talking about your feelings and opinions is also a comfort. Thank you for caring and for talking and doing something that truly matters for yourself and someone else.

WHERE DO I SEND MY FINISHED QUILT?

For more information on where your finished ABC Quilt is most needed, send a stamped, self-addressed #10 envelope to

ABC Quilts
Route 4
RR 1, Box 241
Northwood, NH 03261